REVIVING AMERICA'S NATIONAL WILL FOR THE GLOBAL WAR ON TERROR

> … I say to you: that we are in a battle and that more than half of this battle is taking place in the battlefield of the media. And that we are in a media battle in a race for the hearts and minds of our Umma.
>
> —Ayman al-Zawahiri,
> Osama bin Laden's Second in Command

Just as the enemy will fight for the ideological battlefield, the hearts and minds of the American "Umma" will be won or lost also by reaching out to influencers in communities, through local and regional officials, and through the media. The fact that America is a nation at war is evidenced by the commitment of no less than 150,000 (pre and post surge) to 175,000 (surge) in human capital to fight the insurgents and terrorism in Iraq and more than 30,000, until recently, to Afghanistan. It is evident by the amount of news coverage America is receiving, or the lack thereof, that the appetite for the news about the Global War on Terror (GWOT) has waned. A quick search of news coverage about the GWOT shows a consistent decline in media coverage of the Global War on Terror. During the last 20 days of September 2001, the term "GWOT" appeared 31,000 times in news articles. The following month it reached the highest level at 35,700 articles. The news coverage continued with a steady decline through December 2002 when reporting hit a monthly low of 12,700. But as talk of attacking Iraq gained momentum the GWOT coverage rose to over 14,000 in January 2003 and 18,000 in February 2003 with the third highest level of monthly media coverage attained in March 2003 (27,400 articles) when hundreds of U.S. and western journalists embedded with US and Coalition forces for the ground invasion into Iraq. Following the invasion news reporting dipped steadily again with temporary spikes in March 2004, due in part to spectacular attacks against US forces coupled with the discovery of improper treatment of prisoners at Abu Ghraib prison. The second spike was in September 2004 (21,500) when the US election campaign was heating up and debates between the Republican and Democratic candidates touched on the subject of GWOT. Since the day of President Bush's second inauguration, the mention of GWOT in news has declined dramatically to just over 120,000 articles for all of 2008 and abruptly hit bottom with no more than 2,900 articles the first 20 days in January. There was no media mention of GWOT the full month of February following the inauguration.[2] In short, America is aware that the nation is at war but is generally apathetic to this fact because the military is "taking care of it." The media's attention has refocused on domestic issues, like the economy, because this is where the public's attention has gone. Following September 11, 2001 the apparent intent of President Bush was to reassure the American people that they had the world's best military and could be confident that it will take care of the enemy. He was successful in easing the minds of the public and letting them get back to life as usual.

When news is reported about Iraq or Afghanistan it is usually along two lines: numbers of casualties caused by a spectacular attack on US forces; and political rhetoric about how soon we can withdraw from Iraq. The latter is a moot point for now since the Maliki government passed the Status of Forces Agreement containing the stipulation that U.S. forces would be withdrawn by 31 December 2011.[3] Bemoaning the fact that news about the GWOT is not being reported in a more positive light is in no way meant to imply that media organizations have a perceived slant. Nor is it entirely the media's fault there is a lack of military leadership publicly commenting to routinely inform the nation about the progress of the war effort. It is not the inherent responsibility of the media to supplant other news of the day to cover military actions in Iraq or Afghanistan or to give air time to Army senior leaders to discuss the war. There are always going to be competing demands for news airtime. The television news organizations all follow a similar process to determine what will be the focus for their news that day. It is a competitive business and if the Army wants to be a part of the news it has to fight for air time, or gray space in the case of newspapers.[4]

There is a shared responsibility of commanders and the Public Affairs community to aggressively seek out opportunities to tell the Army story and to prepare the senior leaders with targeted and specific messages. Facts in the news environment today do not speak for themselves; commanders must state the facts and let the media interpret the facts

In the pages that follow, this paper compares and contrasts the communication goals and strategies of WWII and the GWOT in order to draw conclusions about shortcomings today. These include a lack of focused messaging about GWOT; lack of oversight; and a lack of redundancy in executing the Army's Strategic Communications 3+2+1 program. This paper will offer a case study in executing the Army's 3-2-1 program, with conclusions about future strategies. The intent is to help prepared Army senior leaders engage America with the objective truth and help shake off their apathy, succeed in the fight for the gray space, and thereby help America rekindle its resolve to win the war.[5]

World War II and the Global War on Terror

Before September 11, 2001, the last attack suffered on American soil was at the hands of the Japanese at Pearl Harbor on December 7, 1941. In the days following the attack President Franklin D. Roosevelt proclaimed that it was "a day that will live in infamy." The attack on US military facilities and personnel in Hawaii were devastating and were primarily against military targets. The Japanese sneak attack was not specifically directed against civilians and the force that struck was a military force who wore uniforms and were sponsored by a recognized state. The loss of military life and equipment was devastating: "2,403 dead, 188 destroyed planes and a crippled Pacific Fleet that included 8 damaged or destroyed battleships."[6] The Japanese who attacked Pearl Harbor were an enemy who could be identified and could be fought against. America had other enemies besides Imperialist Japan but the sneak attack on Pearl Harbor was the event that awoke a sleeping giant and roused her to join her allies. By the end of the day following the attacks on December 7th, everyone across America knew of the event. This was going to change the nation forever. U.S. enemies also included Hitler's Nazi Germany and Mussolini's Fascist Italy.

Once America entered WWII, every American had a job to do to support the war effort. In 1941, the nation joined an ongoing war with a much bigger stake in the game by way of finances, people, jobs, goods, and services. Rationing of gas, tires, and food were constant reminders of the common sacrifice being made. Victory gardens were reminders that war had not ended. Troop trains, recruiting stations, USO centers in towns across the country were an ever-present sign of the war. U.S. Savings Bonds were sold. Women replaced men in the workplace as men enlisted or were drafted into military service. Nearly every family had someone in uniform or knew someone who was in uniform during WWII. A new phenomenon arose: women joined the Women's Army Corps (WAC). This was a new generation and a new era for America sparked by the unprovoked attacks on Pearl Harbor and it was sustained and given its steel by the effective communications strategy led by the president and his effective use of the "bully pulpit." Hollywood, too, joined in the war effort by producing movies that stirred patriotism and loyalty to the U.S.

The government's efforts to manage information and manage public perceptions of the conduct of the war were extensive and effective during World War II. President Roosevelt wasted no time establishing two new government organizations in 1942: one to lead the censorship efforts, i.e., the Office of Censorship[7] (OC) and a second, the Office of War Information[8] (OWI), to employ the help of Hollywood to make films that would encourage America to stay the course. OC was led by a former Associated Press editor, Byron Price, who convinced the president that the news organizations could censor themselves. For instance, when President Roosevelt's health would have most likely been the top news, there was a collective decision not to report on it because it was believed that it would be bad for morale and give the enemy an unfair advantage against the U.S. It was used to control the news in personal letters going home from the front lines and going to the front lines from home. The government agencies charged with enforcing censorship took their jobs very seriously. "In August 1942 a news columnist received a stern warning from the U.S. government because she described the weather during a trip she took with her husband. Eleanor Roosevelt promised not to do it again."[9]

In reality, censorship was another way to control the news going out and coming into the U.S., ensuring, as much as possible, that the news was positive and encouraging. It was as important to control public perceptions as to keep troops safe. The premise was to ensure troops remained safe. New government agencies were authorized and organized to ensure that public received the right perspective on news from the front lines. Their purpose was intended to: 1.) confirm that the news from home going up to the front lines was upbeat and encouraging; and, 2.) be certain the news coming home did not compromise the safety of the troops in harm's way.

Over 14,000 censorship office employees read all the daily news content asking the same question journalists asked before publishing their stories: "Is this information I would like to have if I were the enemy?" Price claimed that only one time during WWII did any US news agency intentionally break the rules.[10] The OWI director, Elmer Davis, was in charge of publicly released information about the war effort for domestic readership. He also established a foreign news office overseas which began a large scale propaganda effort led by Robert Sherwood, who was a renowned Pulitzer Prize winning author. Sherwood was also noted as a speech writer for President Roosevelt. By 1944, near the end of the war, the OWI, of which Congress had been severely critical, was underfunded and spent most of its resources in the foreign effort.[11] Nevertheless, journalists and Hollywood supported the president in making news from America as positive and upbeat as possible. They avoided mentioning events or circumstances that would make the United States vulnerable to the enemy.

This effort to manage public information extended to censoring mail.[12] Mail was censored before it came into the US and before it left to go to the troops on the front lines. The Army introduced "V-Mail" ostensibly because it was a better way to reduce pay loads of bulk mail going to and from theater. Letters were put on microfilm and flown into and out of theater. Once the microfilm arrived, it was transferred back onto paper copies and sent to their final destinations from v-mail sites all across the US and in locations throughout theater. This reportedly reduced the amount of time it took for news from home to get to the front from 2 weeks to a matter of 3 or 4 days.[13] Censorship was widely accepted as necessary during WWII, and the media cooperated with very effective self-policing, but today's media environment is starkly different. If the government decided to start an organization with the sole purpose of censorship there would be an outrage of tsunamic proportion.

On September 11, 2001, America again became the victim of an unprovoked attack. Since that day our nation has been at war, although not everyone agrees, and that is where part of the problem rests. "Part of the educational failure of the past seven years is explaining the kind of war we're in and why the fight is in our national interest to win."[14] There are parallels between WWII and our current war. Both attacks were unprovoked and produced national outrage and commitment to take the fight to the perpetrators. Both of these wars are global in nature. Our enemies then and now are motivated by ideology. Our enemies believe they are right and anything they can do to defeat us is justified. There are no boundaries to violence in their cause for victory.

While every American was engaged in some way with the war during WW II, the opposite is true today. America's financial investment today in the global war has not caused any to miss a cup of coffee at their favorite café. No one in America has gone without the normal luxuries they have enjoyed for the last seven years. During WWII the

U.S. Gross Domestic Product (GDP) spent on the war effort peaked at almost 38 %[15], while during the GWOT the U.S. government has only spent about 4 % of the GDP on the war effort. In 1944, at the height of US military involvement in the war, the nation fielded a force that at its height exceeded 16,000,000[16] in uniform out of a population of just over 138,000,000 over 11 % of the total U.S. population. [17] Today the US population is over 303,000,000 with a total military strength just over 2,200,000. This equates to less than 1 % of the U.S. population engaged in the war. In 1941, the nation entered WWII during a depression with unemployment at or near 15 %. In 2001, when the U.S. entered the GWOT the economy was doing quite well and the unemployment rate fluctuated at around 6 %.[18] Fewer Americans today know a uniformed service member personally, making the war more remote and distant, causing military service to seem a less viable alternative for employment.

The U.S. role in WWII lasted from December 1941 to August 1945, just under four years. The current war has lasted twice as long and there seems to be no end in sight. Americans and the American media are tired of the war. Yet author James Carafano concludes that the government's leaders (and this includes the senior military leaders) need to begin the difficult task of changing public opinion and reminding America that the war is not over and the "stakes in this war extend to their lives, liberty, and future prosperity."[19] Unfortunately this voice and this message is not widely accepted or believed. The predominant contrarian view of the U.S. stakes in Iraq is projected by The CATO Institute's William A. Niskanen: "It is much less clear that we have an important stake in the outcome of the several civil wars in Iraq."[20] Views are divided on what the stakes are in Iraq. The dilemma this poses to the national will is more a question of how military leaders today can convince America that winning the long war is important.

While military service during WWII became the alternative to unemployment, less than 1 percent of adults between 18 and 24 years of age are even eligible to join the military today. There is no draft, and the smaller eligibility pool makes recruiting even more challenging. If U.S. opinion undermines recruiting this pool of eligible recruits will shrink even smaller. The flood of public opinion in America will influence elected officials as they decide what percent of the U.S. budget should be spent on discretionary and nondiscretionary items. And if, as Carafano predicts, the military budget is reduced further and sustained at its current rate of below 6 percent, it will take many years to rebuild the military because of the long term negative impact from underfunding in terms of research and development, recruiting, and retention.

One of the greatest spokespersons for a nation at war is the Commander-in-Chief (CINC); President Barack Obama has a great example to follow in President Franklin D. Roosevelt. During WWII, Roosevelt used the bully pulpit to keep America informed about the war effort. He put his budget where his mouth was by introducing new agencies which unified his efforts to ensure America did not take its eyes off the ball while engaged in a World War on two fronts and communicated his intent and views to Americans. Their most precious commodity was heavily invested in the war effort: fathers, sons, daughters, brothers, sisters, aunts, and uncles. Roosevelt was a master at word pictures and in many of his fireside chats he used illustrations that related to America's strength of resolve and commitment, and her ability to stand in the face of danger. In the opening lines of his September 8, 1943 broadcast he used an illustration of a Midwestern town that was threatened by a flood. The people of that town all joined in the effort to fill sand bags and together they saved the town from certain destruction. He further mused, "To me, that town is a living symbol of what community cooperation can accomplish." The flood he spoke of had been raging for four years and was the many communities of America who would, together, defeat the flood whose waters were beginning to recede. He concluded, "In this war bond campaign we are filling bags and placing them against the flood -- bags which are essential if we are to stand off the ugly torrent which is trying to sweep us all away."[21] The War Bonds program during WWII gave every citizen of all ages a way to directly join the war effort.

In the current war, former President George W. Bush did not create any additional agency with the sole purpose of keeping America informed. He was also not as effective in reminding Americans that they are at war and reinforcing their will to win the long war. When the former president spoke to the nation about GWOT, it was episodically, but the message was consistent—he wanted America to "go about our daily lives" while we were at war. The problem with this message is it did not keep American's attentive to the war and along the way the nation has lost its resolve to win. In today's technologically advanced environment it is merely a matter of imagination to determine the best way to fan the flame of national resolve. The country needs to know that progress is being accomplished by the warriors who are invested in defeating terrorists, liberating nations under repression, and helping to rebuild these nations, while keeping America safe from further attacks on her homeland. The most far-reaching technology of WWII was the radio. Today there is so much more at the disposal of the CINC, yet the weekly radio broadcast was the main venue which President Bush chose to inform the American public.[22] The problem with radio on Saturday is that traditionally Saturday provides the lowest listening audience for radio in America. The weekly radio broadcast is a good concept and if it followed a highly-popular program like NPR's <u>Click and Clack</u>, the highest rated and most listened to radio program on Saturday mornings, it might have had a better following.[23] Whether radio, television, or some other medium, the issue remains that it is necessary to get the right message to the American people and often. Facts and data that are easy to digest in a ten-minute window and former president Bush and many of our senior government officials did not and do not excel in the art of presenting facts that Americans will find relevant and understandable. With such an enduring war as the present one, time is on the side of the enemy.[24] The longer the war lasts, the more challenging it will become to keep America interested and engaged. Nevertheless the President is the most powerful, important, and effective communicator to accomplish this objective.

The effort to gain national will rests with national leadership starting in the White House and working throughout the government which joins the chorus of the military's voice. Regardless of the role and effects of the nation's leaders, the military has an obligation to give the facts voice. In fact, the respect for the military's professional integrity as an institution rises when its leaders communicate the facts upon which their military decisions are based. Strategic level military leadership cannot be seen as opposing political leadership. That would put at risk the constitutional principle of civilian control. But what should be done is to always let the facts speak, then base advice on the facts. In this way, the military offers a factual assessment consistent with its constitutional duty. This communication is done best when it is led by the commander-in-chief, supported by his administration and the officials elected to represent the American people in Washington and supplemented with the military voices.

The Army's 3+2+1 Program

The media environment has changed, even though the stakes are as high today as during WWII. Media support to the point of censorship is not going to happen today because the media is more independent. Enlisting the media to report predominantly human interest stories to gain national will in support of the long war is not likely to occur.[25] The challenge for the Army now is to keep the American people informed about the GWOT. And, it is not the media's problem to solve. It is the responsibility of Public Affairs Officers to rise to the challenge and ensure that each is doing their part, use the assets already available, and enlist their creative imagination to take the offensive in the battle for the attention of the American people. There is help in this challenge for Army PAOs.

The Army Public Affairs Strategic Communication branch has developed a strategy of engagement called "3+2+1: Engagement for Senior Leaders."[26] The program directive states three objectives that must be accomplished each quarter by the Army senior officers and civilians (General Officers and Senior Executive Service civilians):

3 – Talk to non-military community audiences (Outreach Engagements) three times per quarter;

2 - Conduct interviews with commercial media news organization; print, radio and TV broadcast, web, etc. (External Media Engagements) two times per quarter;

1 – Conduct one event with a military audience (Internal Engagement) at least one time per quarter.

The program sets standards for commanders, senior civilians, and their PAOs to engage their audiences with a predetermined regularity every quarter. If just the uniformed users of the 3+2+1 program actually engaged with the intended audiences and media with the regularity prescribed by the program directive, the Army would have over 4,400 internal engagements, 8,800 media engagements, and 13,200 community outreach engagements each quarter. Multiply those numbers times four and you would have a very good outcome, if numbers were the goal. The beauty of this program is in its simplicity and sheer statistical odds of success. But, as of this writing there is thin reporting at best. This program is voluntary, the reporting is sketchy, and there is little evidence of the program's effectiveness or if the program can be effective.

Successful implementation of the 3+2+1 program is accomplished if the order of engagements places community engagements as the highest priority, then the internal audience, and lastly, the media. The target audience is the American people and the direct approach is always better. One can achieve limited success by conducting the requisite engagements in sheer numbers. However, to attain the objective to build and maintain the national will and commitment for the long war, the engagements must be on American's turf and at their convenience.

A closer examination of the program in its current format reveals a few weaknesses that make management of the program, in its current state, unrealistic and difficult. The first weakness is in messaging because, although the 3+2+1 program is online and is linked to the Army Strategic Themes and Messages, the messages include statements on the budget, an all volunteer army, and modernization of the Army."[27] There is not one message that says we are a nation at war. Since the National Military Strategy and the National Security Strategy both state that winning the global war is one of the highest priorities, it would make logical and strategic sense that this should be the Army's top message.

The second weakness of the program is accountability. The program is voluntary and dependent on the senior leader's PAO to report online when the required engagements are completed. This assumes that the PAO will comply and the commanders will support the PAO in implementing the program. However, if there is no enforcement or consequence tied to the program to compel commanders and their PAOs to engage, competing demands and tyranny of the urgent will overtake the PAO and the use will not accomplish the desired outcome.

The assumption is that all PAOs will ensure their senior leaders and commanders will participate and that the PAOs will provide the appropriate feedback to Army Strategic Communications. The truth is that many want to participate but do not. They either do not retrieve the materials that are available online at AKO's PAO Portal to stay on message with other Senior Army leaders, or they find the material irrelevant to their command and make up their own themes and messages. In either case, these valuable tools provided to PAOs are not used effectively and commanders are not speaking on message. The program's merit is in pressing senior leaders to actively, routinely engage with multiple audiences – as happened at Fort Lewis.

The Fort Lewis Model: Community, Media, and the Command

The application of the Army's 3+2+1 Program was used with great success at Fort Lewis under the command of then LTG James Dubik, now retired. To paraphrase the words of Tip O'Neal, "all public opinion is local." Not only is public opinion local, in the case of the military at Fort Lewis, and installations across the continental US, it is public opinion that really matters the most. This is the approach that LTG Dubik took at Fort Lewis during his command of I CORPS from November 2004 until June 2007, when he relinquished command. At Fort Lewis the Public Affairs trident: community relations (outreach), media relations, and command information (internal audience) took on new meaning as LTG Dubik explained his priorities for Public Affairs and gave his command guidance to the Public Affairs Officer.[28]

LTG Dubik's commander's guidance for public affairs emphasized community relations (COMREL) as the center piece. He wanted to revive the community outreach through an existing but, then-inactive, program which had been created in 2000 by GEN James T. Hill, the I CORPS Commanding General, and executed by his PAO, COL Mary Ann Cummings. The program is called "Community Connections" and was originally designed to have each of the Brigade Commanders (13) connect with each of the surrounding communities by attending community meetings, Chambers of Commerce meetings, mayoral events, and Town Hall meetings. They were to make their presence known to assure the community leaders that Fort Lewis would participate in civilian sponsored events in the community. Since 2005 Fort Lewis connections have expanded to 14 communities, adding the Nisqually Native American Tribe in 2008. The overarching goal for "Community Connections" is senior commander's (brigade level) involvement in the surrounding communities. Under GEN Hill the program was very

15

successful and won the 2001 Army Community Relations Award for Excellence.[29] Since 2001, following GEN Hill's departure from the I CORPS, the program experienced a decline in relevance, use, and command emphasis until LTG Dubik took command at I CORPS and revived it in 2005.[30]

The public affairs challenge was to identify venues (audiences), themes, and execution. The outreach plan stated that presidents of all four-year institutions of higher education would be invited to visit Fort Lewis for a tour and hear briefings about the post's successful environmental programs, Soldier Wellness programs, and technical training programs. The College and University invitations were extended to University of Puget Sound (UPS), Pacific Lutheran University (PLU), Seattle University (SU), University of Washington (UW), and Evergreen College. The other outreach efforts to inform community leaders and opinion leaders included Rotary Clubs, Lions Clubs, local and regional Veteran Service Organizations, Chambers of Commerce, mayors, state and national representatives, Governor Christine Gregoire and spouse, Senators Patty Murray and Maria Cantwell. Key community events provided a positive image of the military and invited the community to hear and see the Army Soldier today: the Seattle Sea-Fair Festival, Memorial Day Parades, Veterans Day activities, and 4th of July Celebrations throughout the Greater Puget Sound Area.

Command information and media relations were supporting elements of the Fort Lewis' Public Affairs program. The Public Affairs vision was to "create an effects-based and message-driven culture of engagement."[31] The statement was short, succinct, and stated clearly what had to be accomplished: engage the external and internal community while engaging the media.

Community Connections Locations

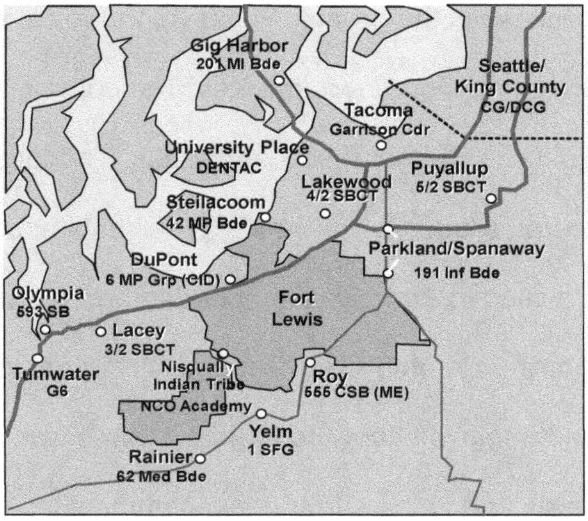

Figure 1: Fort Lewis Community Connections Region by Brigade Command Area of Responsibility.

Fort Lewis public engagements were built upon the overarching theme, or understanding, that "America is a Nation at War." To get the intended audiences to listen to these messages it was imperative to address the elephant in the living room, the environment. The environment would continue to be a distraction unless it was addressed. By addressing the issue, the command acknowledged a shared interest with community members and could build on that link to introduce other community priorities, e.g., why training was so critical to success for the units at Fort Lewis in fighting the long war. The themes at Fort Lewis from 2004 to 2007 were:

1. America is a Nation at War.

2. Our Soldiers are the best Stewards of our Land.

3. America's Army: Who We Are, What We Do, We Are Grounded in Values

These themes were central to outreach to the communities and their leaders in the greater Puget Sound Area. The outreach efforts were targeted, specific, and deliberate. The primary issues in the greater Puget Sound Area, environment and deployment, are the very things Fort Lewis did well. The command sought to ensure the communities were well informed about these successes. The target audiences for the environmental aspect were college and university presidents and deans. Every college and university that was invited to Fort Lewis responded positively to the invitation and either came to the post or the Commanding General (CG) went to them. In each instance, the college leadership left knowing that Fort Lewis was a good steward of the environment, on Fort Lewis and in the surrounding communities as well. These environmental messages were backed with facts and graphic proof of the money spent on cleaning the environment, protecting endangered species, and cleaning up noise and air pollution. The briefing usually included an aerial photo of Fort Lewis in color. The view from several thousand feet above the earth looking down at the post showed how the area outside the post was well developed and did not have much green space. Inside the boundaries of the post the picture showed a different story. The land was green and the developed areas were minimal and concentrated to two cantonment areas or Garrisons. The green spaces are the areas the soldiers trained in and maintained because that is all the land we will ever have for training. If maintained well the land can continue to be used for training. Evergreen College President, Dr. Les Purce responded to his visit: "I was very impressed with the program" and for his Environmental Department to see this program and learn from what Fort Lewis did.[32]

Academic leaders were recognized for their influence on opinions and ideas on campus and within the Puget Sound community. Their understanding of what the post, and more importantly the Army, is doing in the area of improving and sustaining the environment is a small and often overlooked but critical part of the bigger picture in the surrounding community footprint. Also, they must understand the need for American resolve to sustain the long war. The I CORPS and Fort Lewis Commander successfully tied in the environmental messages while reminding the University educators that their nation is at war.

It was the intent that through the community outreach program these leaders would be exposed to the military, become informed about the military, and became a spokesperson to their community with a more informed opinion about their military. These opinion and community leaders have become the informed voice he envisioned. Mayor Natalie Banks of Roy, WA expressed her appreciation of the Community Connections program. Although the 555th Engineers had many Soldiers deployed to Iraq and Afghanistan, they always had time to give to the local schools, Salmon Festival, Summer Health and Safety Fair, and the Fourth of July Celebration. She was aware of the challenges because the assigned brigade has had a consistent presence in the town's activities.[33] The same holds true in each of the outreach communities. Lacey Police Chief, John Suessman expressed his thanks, "We embrace the military here in Lacey and value our relationship with the fort and the patriots that serve our nation."[34]

The success of the Community Connections Program relies on repetition. The more involved the Brigade Commanders are in their assigned community, the more informed the communities and their leaders and people are about the reality of a nation at war. The Stryker Brigade Combat Teams (SBCT) deploy as whole units. The other brigades deploy as partial units, but all deploy and all have become an integral part of their community. The town of Puyallup, Washington was another community that rallied behind the troops and their families when the 3rd SBCT deployed to Iraq for 15 months in spring 2007. The mayor stayed in email contact every week with the commander. The town's people sent packages, supported families at Fort Lewis from the Brigade during the deployment and one of the local journalists was embedded with the unit for their first few weeks of deployment.

The tie-in with community spills over into the media as well. The *Tacoma News Tribune* (TNT) was and remains a strong supporter of the Post. The reporter who deployed with 3rd SBCT reported for the *TNT* and had a specific blog site set up for the community to keep them posted daily on the progress of their unit.

The media is the second branch of the trident of Public Affairs for Fort Lewis and they are just as vital as community. *Seattle Post-Intelligencer* reporter Mike Barber stated it very well when he asserted that the Fort Lewis leadership understood media "weren't the enemy and shared a common interest in wanting to tell the Army's story, especially now in wartime."[35] From local hometown to the Gannett Corporation Newspaper, Fort Lewis enjoyed a good relationship with the media and much of it is attributed to the Commander. LTG Dubik was involved in direct engagements on a regular basis with the media, starting with a media roundtable with all regional media from Seattle to Olympia, including TV, print, and radio. In December 2005, LTG Dubik invited the regional media into his home for the first of many editorial boards.

The point at which LTG Dubik felt he had gained the media's credibility was when he was asked to write the Memorial Day Opinion piece for the Seattle Times. Reading the commentary provides unusual insight into the mind of LTG Dubik. On 28 May, 2006 the Seattle Times published this letter in its entirety without editing one word.[36]

The importance of community for the military is much more meaningful today than it was during WWII. Prior to and during WWII the marriage rate and birth rates were much lower due to economic restraints of the depression and the deployment level during the war.[37] Today 51 percent of the Soldiers in the Army are married. Of those married, nearly 10 percent are females and of these nearly four in 10 are married to other military members.[38]

The measure of performance at Lewis was in part based on numbers of engagements with the community leaders, community groups, college and university leadership, and media interactions. The Community Connections program was command directed and it served as a forcing function to ensure the Brigade Commanders were engaging with communities and the feedback mechanism for these engagements was a quarterly briefing the brigade commanders provided to the CG.

The measures of effectiveness were the direct feedback received from the elected officials, community leaders, and college and university presidents with whom the command engaged. Their feedback was important to ensure the messages were received correctly. That is why repetition was so important in the community program. It takes several times hearing and seeing a message before it can be adequately understood and processed by the receiver. From November 2004 until May 2007 the Community Relations section at Fort Lewis processed, on average, over 350 external requests for speakers at locations throughout the Puget Sound region annually. The media section annually responded to or provided over 1,500 interviews, requests for information, and media engagement opportunities on the post and other areas within the region. The post had three primary reporters who regularly attended events at the post and who interviewed leaders and subject matter experts for stories they wrote about events, activities, or programs at Fort Lewis.[39]

As with all models, there are always some design flaws. The model at Fort Lewis had one notable imperfection: metric tracking.[40] During more than two years at the post the PA team did track media and other events, and recorded when media reported on those events, and gathered feedback from the communities. However, there was no central repository into which the data was archived and periodically reviewed to determine whether the message sent was hitting the intended audience with the desired effect. But, the command team was a learning, growing organization and, gained a valuable lesson from this flaw: always measure progression. With that in mind when the commander and his PAO deployed to Iraq in 2007 they took the lesson they learned at Fort Lewis and exported it to Iraq adding the dimension of metrics. The next few charts depict the Multinational Security Transition Command-Iraq (MNSTC-I) media engagement tracking process.

Exported to MNSTC-I:

In contrast to I CORPS and Fort Lewis with 14 separate local communities, MNSTC-I's command was diverse and comprised over 2,000 U.S. and coalition forces and contractors from hundreds of towns and cities across the U.S. and seven European nations. The intent with the engagements at MNSTC-I was for senior leaders to engage across a wide spectrum of media from the American and other western media through outlets residing in Baghdad to reach communities in America and Europe. This gave the command reach back to the countries from which the senior leaders came and where they would return. This approach worked and allowed the command to reach a wide and diverse audience. This connected MNSTC-I with its intended audiences in America and Europe. It was the Commanders personal involvement that set the climate to allow this connection. It was the senior leaders desire to tell their story that allowed them to connect with their communities.

Figures 2 and 3 track the command's senior leaders impact in news reports based on the leaders' media engagements. What these figures show is the importance of repetition in messaging. The first seven months were marked by low numbers of media reports, reflecting a low return on the leaders' investment in public engagements.

MEDIA HITS for MNSTC-I GOs, SESs, and PAO
April – December 2007

Senior Leaders and SMEs	Position	April	May	June	July	August	September	October	November	December
LTG Dubik	CG MNSTC-I	7	6	13	35	93	139	23	288	275
BG Gledhill (*)	DCG MNSTC-I					2	5	5	233	103
Mr. Kershaw (*)	MOD-TT									
Mr. Maguire	INT-TT								5	1
MG Jones	CPATT						11	6	0	
BG Phillips	DCG CPATT					1	37	25	1	11
BG Weighill (*)	CG MOI-TT								2	
BG Swan	CG CMATT							13	8	9
BG Kahle	DCG CMATT					1	15			
BG McManus (*)	CG JHQ-TT									
BG (P) Allardice	CG CAFTT	1			2	9	5	2	3	5
LTC Williams	MNSTC-I PAO					154	7	3		22
CAFTT									3	6
Iraqi Army - Corruption							23	76	37	75
CMATT								1		
Iraqi Police - Corruption							29	58	132	49
CPATT								6	2	
Iraqi Ministry of Defence								10	11	10
Iraqi Ministry of Interior								65	13	36
Al Qa'im POE						21	20	5	21	
"impossible to tell exactly how much difference"	LTG Dubik's quotes from the								40	
"Iraq's security forces are improving but..."	21 November MNF-I Press								20	
"The speed of withdrawals has been tied to impr	Conference & Mr Tait								20	
San Diego Fire Donations								75	6	
GAO Report					4	292	137	44	41	
Totals By Month		8	6	13	46	622	601	725	1579	844

Figure 2: Number Media Reports on MNSCT-I, April – December 2007, by Name of General Officer, SES and PAO Speakers.

*MEDIA HITS for MNSTC-I GOs, SESs, and PAO Januray – March 2008

Senior Leaders and SMEs	Position	January	February	March
LTG Dubik	CG MNSTC-I	416	33	301
Brig Torrens-Spence (*)	DCG MNSTC-I	2	1	0
MG Ponpegnani	NTM-I	2	1	0
Mr Kershaw (*)	MOD-AT	0	0	0
Mr Bond	INT-TT	0	0	13
MG Jones	DoIA	0	3	0
BG Phillips	CPATT	0	0	1
Brig Thomas	MOI-TT	0	0	0
BG Swan	DDA/CAATT	0	0	13
Brig Schmidt	DoIA	0	0	0
Brig Dunn (*)	JHQ-AT	0	0	0
BG Bash/ MG Allardice	CAFTT	22	12	132
LTC Williams	PAO	0	1	128
Iraqi Air Force		2792	418	376
CAFTT		21	1	35
Iraqi Army - Corruption			1850	2162
CAATT		0	2	32
Iraqi Police - Corruption		0	256	600
Carabinieri		2507	50	500
Iraqi Ministry of Defence		53	1782	783
Iraqi Ministry of Interior		47	282	672
"huge progress in many	LTG Dubik Quote			166
"But we're not free of	LTG Dubik Quote			166
"will take years to	LTG Dubik Quote			128
Besmaya		63	19	337
MNSTC-I		27	33	166
* Require Nation Approval				
Totals By Month		5866	4699	6723

*Media Hits: These numbers are based on how many articles were written from interviews, press conferences, press releases, and events covered by media.

Figure 3: Number Media Reports on MNSCT-I, April – December 2007, by Name of General Officer, SES and PAO speakers.

The figures, above, reflect senior leader engagements. Additionally, soldiers of every rank engaged America through newspaper and TV news interviews and news releases to their hometowns -- totaling more than 4,000 impressions. The media outreach program was planned to engage the wide spectrum of American and Western media representatives working in Baghdad, who in turn reached back to the US communities where soldiers lived and would return. The soldiers' interest in telling their stories, and their fellows soldiers' stories, was complemented by a command climate that supported those efforts. The leaders create that positive command climate through the role modeling, mentorship, and positive feedback that reflect the commander's recognition that strategic communication is a commander's responsibility.

From November 2007 through March 2008 the repetition and consistency of messages translated to an increase of articles written about MNSTC-I of 1000 percent. Key messages the command wanted to communicate, e.g., "Iraq's security forces are beginning to improve but much remains to be done," and "Iraqi's are making huge progress in many areas," were beginning to consistently appear in these articles. The media captured what the commanders spoke about during battlefield circulations (short trips to areas where Iraqi Security Forces were training)[41], press conferences, and interviews.

MNSTC-I Individual Senior Leader Media Engagements From 1 Oct 07 to 6 Apr 08

Communicator	Directorates	Position	Battlefiled Circulations	Press Conferences	Interviews	TOTALS
LTG Dubik	CMD	CG MNSTC-I	8	10	43	61
Brig Torrens-Spence	GRP	DCG MNSTC-I	4	1	12	17
MG Pompegnani	NTM	NTM-I	2	2	5	9
BG Swan	Defense Affairs	DDA/CAATT	8	2	18	28
Mr Kershaw	Defense Affairs	MOD-AT	0	0	3	3
Brig Dunn	Defense Affairs	JHQ-AT	0	0	0	0
BG Bash/MG Allardice	Defense Affairs	CAFTT	4	4	10	18
MG Jones	Interior Affairs	DoIA	1	2	16	19
Brig Schmidt	Interior Affairs	DoIA-DCG	1	1	4	6
BG Phillips	Interior Affairs	CPATT	7	3	29	39
Brig Thomas	Interior Affairs	MOI-AT	0	1	6	7
Mr Bond	FCT	INT-TT	0	0	0	0
RADM Winters	FCT	INCTF-TT	0	0	0	0
MG Smith	FCT	SAO	0	1	2	3
Standard: 1-2-3 Quarterly		TOTALS	35	27	148	210

Figure 4: MNSTC-I Senior Leader Engagements Divided into Three Categories: Battlefield Circulation, Press Conference, And Interview.

When LTG Dubik went to Iraq to command MNSTC-I he used the same standard but applied to three specific but different venues: (1) battlefield circulations, (2) press conferences, and (3) interviews per quarter. Figure 4 shows the three areas of concentration for media attention, and how the command performed over time in gaining media coverage, and eventually the desired end state of delivering the commands messages to the American and European audiences. The bottom left-hand corner of this figure states the standard (1-2-3) which means each senior leader will conduct one press conference, two battlefield circulations, and three interviews with media quarterly.

The program Army Strategic Communications developed is versatile and adaptable. It worked at Fort Lewis focusing on community, command, and media. In Iraq it will work with a focus on reaching audiences through engaging the media on training trip, press conferences, and interviews. The key to using the program is adapting it to connect with the intended audience. There is a great deal of work in finding the right audiences, identifying the key themes and messages, and applying the most important factor, command emphasis.

What this method did at Fort Lewis to connect the command with the community also worked in Iraq to connect the MNSTC-I with the American and European audiences providing the facts about what is relevant, engaging the audience in a conversation about the mission and reinforcing why the military needs to have their nations resolve to win the long war.

Conclusion

While America has been at war for over seven years, somewhere along the way it lost the resolve and national will to stay engaged in the global war on terror.

Too, it should be apparent that the military might and the voice of the military leadership alone is not going to regain the attention of America, this requires the full effort of the Commander in Chief, the support of government leadership, and the military speaking collectively to the American people to earn their attention.

And, for the military to reach America it must start locally. The Community Connections program was the method that worked at Fort Lewis, nested in the Army's 3+2+1 Program. The command from MNSTC-I found that while in Iraq the program designed by Army strategic communications also worked. Along the way the Lewis model found flaws that were corrected when exported into the Iraqi theater. The model, with modified design changes, resulted in combining effective themes and messages with planned engagements which kept America engaged in the long war.

The desire is that commanders and PAOs learn from the Fort Lewis and MNSTC-I models and apply these lessons learned to improve strategic communications across the Army while keeping America engaged in the long war, one community at a time.

Endnotes

[1] John Moore, "America: At war or at the mall?", February 22, 2007, http://www.murdoc online.net/archives/004584.html (accessed March 12, 2009).

[2] "Google News Archives – Timeline," http://news.google.com/archivesearch?q=global +war+on+terror&num=10&as_ldate=2009/01&as_hdate=2009/01&scoring=t&hl=en&nav_num= 100 (accessed February 16, 2009) This is a Google navigational tool to track media coverage of issues and items in a specific grouping which depicts a graphic representation of that news coverage over time.

[3] Barrack Obama, "Remarks of President Barack Obama – Responsibly Ending the War in Iraq," February 27, 2009, http://www.whitehouse.gov/ the_press_office/Remarks-of-President-Barack-Obama-Responsibly-Ending-the-War-in-Iraq/ (accessed March 5, 2009).

[4] At CBS News this past fall during the New York City trip, a small group of Army War College students had the opportunity to meet with a senior official of CBS News in her studio office and discuss the news cycle. One student asked her a pointed question about how news is

determined to be news. She revealed that the news cycle for the day starts early in the morning and the stories from about 1,200 to 12 or 13 by 9:30 a.m.

[5] James M. Dubik, e-mail message to author, February 15, 2009. LTG James Dubik commanded I CORPS, November 2004 to May 2007 and MNSTC-I, June 2007 to July 2008.

[6] Walter Lord, "Attack at Pearl Harbor," 1957, http://www.eyewitnesstohistory.com/pearl.htm (accessed February 7, 2009).

[7] "The National Archives; Records of the Office of Censorship," 1934, http://www.archives.gov/research/guide-fed-records/groups/216.html (accessed February 8, 2009).

[8] "The National Archives; Records of the Office of War Information," 1941, http://www.archives.gov/research/guide-fed-records/groups/208.html (accessed February 8, 2009). The United States Office of War Information (OWI) was a U.S. government agency created during World War II to consolidate government information services. It operated from June 1942 until September 1945. It coordinated the release of war news for domestic use, and, using posters and radio broadcasts, worked to promote patriotism, warned about foreign spies and attempted to recruit women into war work. The office also established an overseas branch which launched a large scale information and propaganda campaign abroad.

[9] Martin Smith, "The Perilous Fight: Censorship," February 23, 2003, http://www.pbs.org/perilousfight/home_front/censorship/ (Accessed February 7, 2009).

[10] Ibid.

[11] J. M. Brown, "Biography: Robert E. Sherwood, 1965, http://www.infoplease.com/ce6/people/A0844885.html (accessed February 12, 2009).

[12] "World War II Encyclopedia," http://www.skylighters.org/encyclopedia/vmail.html (access February 7, 2009).

[13] Ibid.

[14] James M. Dubik, e-mail message to author, February 15, 2009.

[15] Steven M. Kosiak, *Analysis of Proposals to Allocate Four Percent of GDP to Defense* (Washington, DC: Center for Strategic and Budgetary Assessments, September 9, 2008), 3, http://www.csbaonline.org/4Publications/PubLibrary/B.20080909.Analysis_of_Propos/B.20080909.Analysis_of_Propos.pdf (accessed February 7, 2009).

[16] "History Shots: U.S. Army Divisions in World War II," January, 2009, http://www.historyshots.com/ usarmy/backstory.cfm (accessed February 7, 2009).

[17] Wendell Cox Consultancy, "Demographia, US Population From 1900," 2001, http://www.demographia.com/db-uspop1900.htm (accessed February 16, 2009).

[18] "Department of Defense Active Duty Military Personnel by Rank/Grade," August 31, 2007, http://siadapp.dmdc.osd.mil/personnel/MILITARY/rg0708.pdf (accessed February 7, 2009).

[19] James J. Carafano, Baker Spring, and Mackenzie M. Eaglen, "Four Percent for Freedom: Maintaining Robust National Security Spending," (Washington DC, The Heritage Foundation, April 10, 2007), 2, http://www.heritage.org/Research/NationalSecurity/upload/em_1023.pdf (accessed February 7, 2009).

[20] William A. Niskanen, CATO @ Liberty, Morbid Comparisons," (Washington DC, The CATO Institute, April 19, 2007), http://www.cato-at-liberty.org/2007/04/19/morbid-comparisons/ (accessed February 23, 2009).

[21] "Fireside chats of Franklin D. Roosevelt," http://www.mhric.org/fdr/fdr.html (accessed on 12 February 2009).

[22] "Pew research Center's Project for Excellence in Journalism, Radio Audience Trends 2006," March 13, 2006, http://www.journalism.org/node/836 (accessed February 7 2009). According to this report and other sources they used in this study (Arbitron, and Edison Media Research) over 82 percent of those surveyed would still listen to traditional radio as much in the future as they do now. This number is down from as few years ago as 1998 when the number of traditional radio listeners topped at over 95 percent.

[23] http://www.nytimes.com/2008/06/29/arts/television/29jens.html [Click and Clack have a following of over 4.3 million listeners every Saturday morning to more than 600 radio stations.]

[24] Based on discussions with LTG Dubik and emails regarding the military's responsibility to remind America we are still at war.

[25] http://www.pbs.org/perilousfight/home_front/censorship/ [Accessed 7 February 2009]

[26] https://www.us.army.mil/suite/portal/index.jsp; Access to this website requires the user to have an AKO account and register for the AKO Public Affairs portal.

[27] https://akocomm.us.army.mil/2008scg/Strategic_Themes.pdf [Accessed 7 February 2009]

[28] The author was the PAO for Lieutenant General James M. Dubik from June 2005 through May 2008. From June 2005 to April 2007 the author served at Fort Lewis as the I CORPS CGs PAO. In April 2007 he deployed to Iraq to serve LTG Dubik as the MNSTC-I PAO.

[29] The 2001 Award Submission for Army Public Affairs Community Relations Award, p 6-7.

[30] From an email exchange with Mike Barber, Seattle Post-Intelligencer, Seattle, WA, military news reporter, dated 11 February 2009, 7:59 pm.

[31] The author was the PAO for Lieutenant General James M. Dubik from June 2005 through May 2008. From June 2005 to April 2007 the author served at Fort Lewis as the I CORPS CGs PAO. In April 2007 he deployed to Iraq to serve LTG Dubik as the MNSTC-I PAO.

[32] Les Purce, e-mail message to author, February 24, 2009. Also, based on comments he gave during his visit to Fort Lewis, Washington, in March 2006.

[33] Natalie Banks, e-mail message to author, February 11, 2009. Natalie Banks is the Mayor of Roy Township, Washington.

[34] John Suessman, e-mail to author, February 12. 2009. John Suessman is the Commander of the Lacey, Washington police department.

[35] Mike Barber, e-mail to author, February 11, 2009. Mike Barber is a reporter at the Seattle Post-Intelligencer, Seattle, WA, and reports on military news.

[36] James M. Dubik, "America at war on Memorial Day," May 28, 2006, http://seattletimes. nwsource.com/html/opinion/2003021649_sunmemorial28.html (accessed February 15, 2009). This commentary was written by LTG Dubik for the Seattle Times. It was written while the general and his command were on exercise in Thailand and his revisions included input from Gen (Retired) Shalikashvili, BG Vincent Brooks, and Gen (Retired) Gordon Sullivan.

[37] "Wikipedia, Post-World War II Baby boom," October 22, 2004, http://en.wikipedia. org/wiki/Post-World_War_II_baby_boom#Marriage_rates (accessed February 15, 2009).

[38] Betty D. Maxfield, "Army Profile," (Washington, DC: Headquarters, Department of the Army, G-1, Chief Office of Army Demographics, September 15, 2004), 4, http://www.armyg1. army.mil/HR/docs/demographics/FY04%20Army%20Profile.pdf (accessed February 15, 2009)

[39] Joe Piek, e-mail to author, October 20, 2008. Joe is the Community Relations and Media Chief at Fort Lewis. He provided the facts and data from Fort Lewis regarding numbers of engagements with regard to community and media events from July 2005, which is when he started working in this position, through April 2007 when the PAO left Fort Lewis to deploy to Iraq. Joe can be reached at: (253) 967-0155.

[40] The author has received email feedback from the Mayors of Steilacoom (Ron Lucas) and Roy (Natalie Banks), Puyallup Chamber of Commerce, Lacey Police Chief John Suessman, Seattle PI reporter Mike Barber, Seattle Times reporter Hal Bernton, Nisqually Native-American Representative Cynthia Iyall, Army Times reporter Michelle Tan, and NPR reporter (now retired) Steve Krueger. All were thankful for the efforts of the Fort Lewis command to reach into the communities through the Community Connections program. The Seattle Times newspaper editor provided the highest form of flattery allowing LTG Dubik to write the 2006 Memorial Day op-ed for their paper and, as they promised, did not edit anything from it or add anything to it.

[41] Battlefield Circulations were an excellent opportunity to take media to training events where the Iraqi security forces were training and show them firsthand the progress the ISF were making. It also afforded one-on-one time with Iraqi senior leaders who frequently accompanied LTG Dubik and the other generals when conducting these events.